Nurs

A collection of thoughts and
discussions through a pandemic.

From the blog *Blue Girl: Nursing Beyond
the Ward*

Blue Girl

Nursing from Home

Emma Gracie

For my readers. I have been overwhelmed by your support of *Blue Girl: Nursing Beyond the Ward*. While this is a very different book, I hope you enjoy it.

Thank you

x

Introduction

In July 2020 I published my nursing memoir *Blue Girl: Nursing Beyond the Ward*. And I thought that I was done. A little book on Amazon that I expected, after reading advice about self-published books, to bumble along and sell perhaps 250 copies. Just over a year on and over 8500 copies have been bought or downloaded and I remain stunned. I cannot express how grateful I am and extremely surprised I am that people over the world, who have never met me, are interested in reading my story. I have been contacted to speak on the radio, in podcasts and at a rally, have featured in articles in local papers, have my book in a library and have been featured in local promotions. Because of these contacts, I have been able to use my social media as a platform to raise awareness of the *NHS15* campaign, chronic disease and perhaps most importantly to me, County Lines. It's been an astonishing year.

And what has possibly meant the most to me are the wonderful messages from student nurses about to embark on - or nurses who have been struggling with - their careers telling me how much my little memoir has inspired them. It's a lot of work writing, formatting and designing your own book, especially on the ropey old laptop that I used. There were many times I wanted to drop it out of my top window. And yet those messages of support made it more than worth it. If I can inspire just one nurse, encourage them in their journey and help them face work in the morning, then that is all the reward I need.

Once *Blue Girl* was out there, I thought I was done writing. I'd told my past stories and wasn't sure what to do with my blog. However, it wasn't long before new ideas began coming to me. Not tales about the past, but thoughts and discussions about the time we've been living in since the pandemic started. So this little book, that I see as a baby sister to my first one, is very different. It's more topical and is written as a collection of blogs rather than a memoir. Maybe you'll agree with my opinions, maybe not. In many instances I'm not sure what my stance even is. I have written some blogs as a starting point for discussion while others show a stronger take on a subject. I've called it *Nursing from Home* because for much of the pandemic I had to shield, which meant I couldn't fulfil my role as a school nurse in the usual way. I chose to use the time to complete an online counselling course for children and adolescents which enabled me to turn my attention to the mental health of the students. By no means do I consider myself a fully-qualified counsellor, my training was basic and I have virtually no experience in this field, but it certainly gave me the skills I needed to make welfare calls to the children most in need. Instead of seeing the children at school as I normally would, I was able to make phone and video calls from home to keep in touch. The long isolation of home school, especially during winter, meant that they were just relieved to have someone to talk to and listen on a regular basis. I used my experience in yoga to help support them with self-care, mindfulness and calming techniques. Some of the children reported a noticeable difference in their sleep patterns from this which I was thrilled about. Mainly though, they just needed to feel like someone was there. I was very grateful the school set up this system for me and it proved very useful on my return, as I then continued this role for two days a week alongside my more traditional school nurse role.

I should mention that I've included the blog *Dear Mr Johnson* which featured towards the end of my first book. This hasn't been done to cheat you, but because I have since written to Boris Johnson again and included my second letter in chapter two. I didn't feel this book would make sense without the first letter included. I have also included the blog *Strong* which I featured as a bonus blog in later editions of *Blue Girl: Nursing Beyond the Ward*. Since I hadn't written it before publishing my first version, I thought it only fair to include it in chapter three for those early supporters who didn't have it in their copies.

It might be helpful to view this little book like a music album with each chapter like a song. They are each a complete piece on their own so may not flow as a more conventional book might. As with songs on an album, there may be chapters you love and some not so much. But it's my hope that my thoughts and discussions will resonate with you since we have all lived through an unusual time, experiencing the same global event.

Dear Mr Johnson

This letter I wrote before Covid was really a thing in the UK. We'd heard it was in China but hadn't had any cases reported at home. It was even before Boris advised us to wash our hands while singing *Happy Birthday* twice through. Shame that didn't save us.

In September 2020 I was asked to speak at a rally promoting the *NHS15* campaign, a grass roots movement fighting for fair pay and conditions for all NHS staff. I actually read this letter as part of my speech as I felt it was very appropriate to the cause. Even before the pandemic, nurses were at breaking point. Which is why I wrote this to him:

Dear Mr Johnson,

I am sure I don't need to tell you about the challenges our nurses are facing every day of their working lives. They deal with life and death situations, while remaining calm under immense pressure, providing care for all those who cross their path. On second thoughts, maybe I do as your government certainly doesn't seem to be looking out for their wellbeing, so let me lay it out for you.

Between 2016 and 2017 20% more nurses left the register than joined it. 44% of these nurses did not leave because of retirement, they left because they could no longer cope with the intolerable pressure of their working conditions. The goodwill of nurses is being increasingly abused with longer hours, pay rises capped at

1% and, thanks to the marvellous idea of Brexit, fewer nurses in our hospitals.

Fewer nurses on the register means increased fees for those who remain on it. Yes, we have to pay every year to be allowed to care and these fees are constantly rising. Pay is already offensively low considering the work nurses do and this has led to more nurses needing to use food banks.

There has been a marked decrease in the wellbeing of nurses and, while mental health has become an important topic for the general population, it is largely ignored by employers according to the NMC.

When I think back to my training as an inexperienced student nurse, I dealt with extremely heavy issues with absolutely no guidance on how to process them and nobody to talk to. At the age of 19 I witnessed a pregnant woman in her twenties be admitted to A&E with a pulmonary embolism. The team fought for her for as long as possible but tragically neither she nor her baby could be saved. I can still feel the heavy, sombre mood of the ward that day. I was actually instructed by the senior nurse not to talk about it to anyone. We were expected to carry on working as if it were another ordinary day.

On another placement I was told by a mentally disturbed patient that he considered me small enough to fit into a suitcase. He decided he wanted to bury it with me inside in the garden and decorate my grave with Christmas lights. This was the same man who had pushed a pregnant woman down a flight of stairs and who also felt comfortable covering himself in his own faeces in the centre of town. His mind was dark and I found it difficult to know how to be around him. Again, I had nobody to talk to about this experience.

At the age of 22 I was subjected to a young man tossing himself off in front of my desk. I suppose now that would be considered sexual assault and, while the police took it very seriously, I had nobody in the workplace to discuss this distressing incident with.

Even more recently I have been left extremely vulnerable during home visits with one man welcoming me into his home wearing just a towel and another telling me that his 'cock was sore'!

I left ward work long ago opting for general practice instead but over the last fifteen years that has become increasingly high--pressured and we often work with no breaks and an overload of patients. We're lucky if we get to go to the loo. Last year I decided to drastically reduce my work in this field and am now so lucky to predominantly be a school nurse. While I remain busy and deal with an array of issues, some very complex, I have been stunned by how well I am supported in a school compared to the NHS.

In addition to time constraints, limited or faulty equipment, long hours and degrading pay, nurses have an emotional load to bear. We are expected to listen to and solve every patient's problem and in some we really invest ourselves. Working in a school especially has really opened my eyes to inexplicably sad situations that I have no power to change. Truly caring for patients is a huge emotional burden. We don't forget them when we go home.

Nursing is hard. The strain and level of responsibility is hard. So hard that hundreds of nurses have taken their own lives in the last seven years. The suicide rate among nurses is 23% higher than the national average. This is absolutely unacceptable and you must urgently review how our nurses are being treated. They deserve mental health care, shorter shift patterns, regulated breaks and pay that respects their work. If you don't care for them, they won't be able to care for you or your nation.

Hello Again Mr Johnson

I, unsurprisingly, never received any form of response to my letter from Boris. I did however receive a letter from my local MP the late Sir David Amess after sending it to him too. He thanked me for the work nurses do. While this was very kind and I appreciated the time he had taken to contact me, it wasn't going to make a difference to the treatment of nurses. Part of the *NHS15* campaign is to highlight that clapping, while a sweet gesture, doesn't actually help us. This was my second letter to Boris written six months into the pandemic in Britain.

Dear Mr Johnson,

You may remember my previous letter and the book I sent you *Blue Girl: Nursing Beyond the Ward*, which I wrote so that the work of nurses could be understood and appreciated. And by appreciated I mean with more than applause. Since February, when I last wrote to you about the workload of nurses, mental health concerns for NHS staff, poor working conditions, faulty equipment, and offensive pay, our situation has become dire. Nurses and HCAs are continuing to battle the same issues as before but have since worked relentlessly through this pandemic. And they are burning out. Since your time in ICU I expect you now know better than some how tough their job is in the most trying of times. And yet rather than reward us, you have kicked us in the teeth. We are furious that your government has denied us a pay rise and we won't let this rest. Protests are only gaining momentum across the country as increasing numbers of nurses are thinking of leaving the profession they love. You haven't responded to my first letter so let me lay it out for you. Again.

Since March, nurses have worked harder than ever but remain completely undervalued by your government. A recent survey of 42,000 nurses by the RCN revealed that 36% of nurses were considering leaving the profession, an increase from 27% last year. Another study by *Holliblu* found this figure to be a staggering 68%. *Holliblu's* study also found that 50% of nurses feel worried about going to work and are showing signs of anxiety and stress. When asked to score their mental health out of 100, the average score was an extremely alarming 36. With the UK having the second highest death rate among nurses from Covid, it's no wonder anxiety levels are high. 650 health care staff have lost their lives in this fight. And many are holding your government responsible. David Carr, a critical care nurse at St Thomas' hospital where you were treated, told Sky News: 'I'm not a warrior, I'm not a soldier, I don't come to work expecting to die'. You seem to have no grasp on the work nurses do. I was in disbelief when Matt Hancock announced that this year it was going to be possible for nurses to administer the flu vaccine. We have been running these clinics for decades! It is frightening to me that your Health Secretary seems to know so little about how the NHS is actually functioning.

So what would make us feel valued? Unsurprisingly 73% reported that decent pay is a must. 45% are asking for safer working conditions and 43% would like adequate equipment and supplies. All issues I have previously written to you about and ones that are entirely reasonable to expect in order to carry out our jobs safely. During the pandemic a third of nurses have had to work at a higher level than before and guess what? They haven't had a pay increase for the extra responsibility. With a nursing shortage of 40,000 and a possible decrease in nurses joining from overseas due to current travel restrictions you absolutely must do everything in your power to keep the nurses who are giving their all on a daily basis. Morale is at an all-time low. I've said this before and I'll say it again-the suicide rate among female nurses is 23% higher than the national female average. Just let that sink in.

I recently spoke at a protest as part of the *NHSPay15* movement organised by *EssexNHS15* and read out my original letter to you. My local Labour politician Aston Line also spoke and during his superb speech he said that 'For far too long now the Conservatives have relied on the altruism of nurses, paramedics, porters, health care assistants, biomedical scientists and other NHS workers'. He moved the crowd when he said 'I refuse to be content in a world where a full-time working nurse has to rely on food banks to feed their family. None of us should think this is ok.' I ask you Prime Minister, do you? These issues are too crucial to be on the back burner. The time has come for you to back your nurses.

*

I am yet to receive any form of acknowledgment of my letters regarding this campaign. However, I am grateful that through my writing I have been able to raise awareness online and speak about it through various media as mentioned in my introduction. It may be a tiny one but I have played a part in this fight.

Strong

Like most of us, I spent a lot of time during lockdown watching Netflix. One show I really loved (especially after Zac Efron liked one of my tweets about it!) was *Down to Earth*. I was fascinated by one episode in particular and thinking about that led to this blog:

I'm tired. So tired of the 'ideal' body images of both men and women that still bombard us on every platform. And what I am most tired of is that body size, shape and type is still a discussion. Whoever decided that women had to be thin and men had to have a six-pack? And who on earth decided that every woman should contour her face in an effort to lose any individuality? It is so boring that thigh gaps, lack of height, soft bodies, big bums, no boobs, round boobs, abs, dad bods and many other body characteristics are an issue. We are all different to each other and unique to ourselves. And that is OK. In fact more than OK. Our main concern should be internal health, not external appearance.

For a long time during my childhood and teens I struggled with my dance teachers repeatedly calling me a 'big girl' in front of the other dancers. At the time I was 5'3" and about nine stone. A perfectly healthy weight for my height. However, at that impressionable age it instilled in me an unnecessary self-consciousness about my round bum and strong legs. I began watching what I ate at a very early age, dabbled with Slim-Fast, read books like Joan Collins' Beauty Book that encouraged diets such as eating nothing but hard-boiled eggs for three days, and even had a brief encounter with self-induced vomiting after every meal. Thankfully that last one was very short lived but it did nothing to help my developing self-esteem and body image.

At the time the role models were supermodels. Women about seven inches taller than me and probably a stone less than me. A body type I would never be able to accomplish. Then, in 1996 when I was 15 the Spice Girls hit and began to transform the way I viewed myself. They celebrated variety and comfort in one's own body. Sadly though, my favourite one, Geri withdrew and re-emerged about three stone lighter which was confusing and disappointing. But then two other women made the big time and completely changed my impression of beauty. J-Lo and Beyonce. Here were women I could really relate to. Curvy, strong and completely happy with it.

By this point I was a student nurse and had started learning far more about weight than any magazine could teach me. If you have read my book or previous blogs you'll know that I have spent much of my life caring for the elderly. I have made many observations of my patients throughout my career but there are some that I have noticed consistently. One is that the elderly I have nursed always seem younger, stronger and more agile when they have flesh on their bones. I know this sounds obvious. If you're a waif, by the time you reach 90 you have no muscle tone left and need far more assistance than women like Birdie and Flossie who I have previously written about. Women who were both small in height but strong. Perfectly mobile, despite being in their mid to late nineties and, according to old photos, hadn't spent a lifetime trying to weigh as little as possible. From what I could ascertain they enjoyed an active life, drank wine (Flossie's fridge always had at least 3 bottles in it even when she was 98 years old!) and ate from all food groups but, and this is one of my strongest convictions, did it all in moderation.

I recently watched the Netflix show *Down to Earth* starring Zac Efron and Darin Olien. The episode I found most fascinating was the one filmed in Sardinia where it is very common for locals to live past 100. They explored the Blue Zone Diet and it challenged everything Zac had been taught for many years by fitness trainers about a high protein diet. Watching Zac's joy at eating pasta (that he'd made with a Sardinian family) for the first time in a long time was a touching moment. They met a man who, despite being over 100 years old, was active enough to go for three walks a day unaccompanied and who visited his local bar for a glass of wine daily. This sweet man had previously lost his wife and despite missing her deeply still wanted to continue living. He enjoyed simple pleasures and said he'd live 'another 100 years' if he could. The episode confirmed three things that I have seen in so many patients over the years. Firstly, an optimistic and appreciative demeanour is essential for good health, secondly, it is good and one of life's joys to enjoy all sorts of food and drink (but the key is moderation! I can't stress that enough) and lastly, that true health is about more than the here and now. It is so important to consider how you'll fare in years to come.

I have previously written about the health condition I developed at 32 and have now lived with for seven years - Chronic Eosinophilic Pneumonia. I am treated with Prednisolone and a Symbicort inhaler, both a type of steroid. I am only too aware of the potential side effects of these drugs, particularly the Prednisolone, and even though I'm on the lowest dose I've ever been on I know that I have to do everything in my power to combat them. One of the side effects is the risk of reduced bone density so I make sure I include strength yoga in my daily life. I've always done yoga and still can't live without the more Yin style to relax but know I need to keep my bones strong so exercising using my body weight is excellent. But it means I'm not the 'ideal' body shape. My legs are muscular, my bum is round and my arms are bulkier than they used to be. I'm heavier now and don't fit into the size eight jeans I had when I was 20. But I am strong. And I can breathe. My aim now is to stay as strong and well as I can for as long as I can. I want to get old and look after myself like Birdie and Flossie did for so much of their lives. When I first became ill one of the most visible symptoms was weight loss. I weighed about eight stone and I received so many comments about how 'at least I'd lost weight'. Why was this perceived as a good thing?! I'd never felt so terrible in my life and had zero energy. I'm now two stone heavier and feel the best I've felt in seven years.

Of course I understand that some people are naturally very slim. What I'm saying is don't strive to be seven stone if that's not what you are. It makes me so mad that thin is the only female body type that is predominantly celebrated by the media. I remember reading a quote from Kate Moss that said 'Nothing tastes as good as skinny feels'. That type of message is so damaging. And thinness doesn't automatically guarantee good health. I have had patients who are seven stone but have very high cholesterol and are significantly hypertensive. Of course, I'm not saying we should throw caution to the wind and eat McDonalds every day, that would benefit nobody but Ronald, but a life of deprivation won't lead to happiness or good health later on. We need to celebrate beauty in the wonderful variety of people we see. Let's enjoy all that life brings, be healthy and most of all be ourselves.

Be Gentle

This little blog came about after a discussion with my brother one day when we were Christmas shopping. It's something I've never consciously thought about before but I rather liked his observations, so I wrote this:

During one of many Covid-safe walks recently my brother Greg told me that I am one of two people he knows who hasn't had a set 'vision' for life. I jokingly asked if he sees me as a loafer with no aspirations but I knew what he was saying was positive.

We were talking about the past year and how it has affected so many people's plans. It goes without saying that 2020 has turned the world upside down and that, understandably, many have struggled with lockdowns, job changes or losses, relationships or illness. More time spent considering personal situations and futures seems to have been a common thread among people I work with and know personally, with many people making quite drastic changes to jobs and home life. As we talked further Greg explained that he sees my lack of rigid planning as a good approach and that it seems to have made me content in life. I'm aware that I do feel content but I've never considered that this may be, in part, because I failed to make firm plans in my younger years regarding my future. In fact on reflection, much of my life has taken me by surprise. Engaged at 20, married at 22 a baby at 24, another at 27. A third baby never came but maybe that was OK because I didn't have an ideal family in mind, I'm just so grateful for the two children I have.

Aspects of my career have surprised me too. I always knew I wanted to provide care but at the last minute changed from midwifery to nursing. I never expected to be practice nursing at 23, I just didn't think I'd be taken on for lack of experience. Following on I've worked in parish nursing, school nursing and am about to embark on counselling. Again, none of this has been planned, instead I have just grabbed opportunities as they've become available. I never thought to meticulously schedule my life. And now I've had a bit of time to contemplate this, I'm glad I didn't! I've always seen life as a huge jumble of varied experiences. Not all of them good but those are the times that shape us. I never expected to develop a lifelong lung condition at 32 but to quote Ronan Keating 'Life is a rollercoaster, just got to ride it'. Not my taste in music but I agree with the sentiment!

Perhaps a lesson to learn from the pandemic is that a fluid approach to life is key. If we pin hopes on a certain lifestyle or timeline without acknowledging it may not work out, the effects might be damaging to our mental health, our relationships and future choices. If the last nine months have taught us anything it's that we are not really in control. Life can be wonderful. Be gentle with yourself and enjoy all that's in store.

A Better Year

This short blog came to me after Boris announced that households were not to mix last Christmas. I hate to say it but if posts and memes were anything to go by, those of us in certain parts of the South-East had been feeling rather smug about remaining in Tier 2. We were to learn our lesson. Shortly after the tier announcement, that plan was abolished and we too, had to remain indoors with those we live with. I wrote this to try to send some festive cheer to those in my part of the country (including my sisters who were both looking forward to their babies first Christmas) who were feeling very deflated indeed.

So Christmas has been turned on its head like the rest of 2020. Last night's announcement by the government, who seem to have been chasing their tails throughout this whole pandemic, was a real blow to those of us in the South East. Food has been bought, homes have been decorated, presents are under the tree and now we can't share those things with the people we love. But that last sentence is an indicator of how lucky we really are. If we have food, homes to have a tree in, and money to buy gifts we surely are among the richest in the world. And if we have love then we still have the true meaning of Christmas. Whatever your belief, Christmas is about love. And hope. Hope for a better year to come.

If you've read any of my writing before you'll know I have a lot of experience with and great affection for the elderly. One thing that strikes me about the people I know and hold dear who are in their nineties is that they have hope for tomorrow. If they didn't, they'd spend their last years sitting in an armchair waiting for the end. But instead, they persevere and look forward with the resilience that has seen them this far.

Of course it's completely OK for us to be upset and disappointed, that's only natural. But as the little Charlie Brown picture says, maybe this year is the time to reflect on the good in our lives. We've made it nine months living in this madness with people finding new ways to show kindness and support each other. Let's uphold each other any way we can during this festive season. As the Amazon Christmas advert and Strictly winner Bill Bailey have said, 'The show must go on'. It might not be as we know it, or the way we planned but if we stick together with the love that's got us here, we too have hope for tomorrow.

Guilty

I wrote this blog after receiving a number of derogatory comments on an article I was featured in in my local paper. I had used the quote mentioned in *Hello Again Mr Johnson* to raise awareness that some nurses are having to resort to food banks to support their families. One of the comments I reference in this blog is one in which the writer boasts about his own upbringing while insinuating, in the sentence 'want big money? get an education', that nurses don't have an education and have chosen a 'pauper's job'. Of course as he states, we were aware of the pay when we chose this profession. What we could never have expected however, is that with little to no pay rises and our pay failing to keep up with inflation, we are now 20% worse off than we were in 2010. I was incensed by his disrespect of nurses and sincerely hope that if he ever requires medical care he will come to appreciate and understand the professional nature of our work.

I have included his original comment here:

Oh Dearie me, not this again, Yawn.

When you chose a profession the pay has to be a part of your decision, want big money? get an education, want glory? join the army, want free face masks? become a nurse.

We never had food banks when we were a lad, mum & dad worked in education, we never went hungry and enjoyed long holidays abroad, dad always had a new car.

Do a paupers job? then remember your place.

Last Updated: 26th October 2020 12:13 am

This week I received the news I've been waiting for since Christmas - that shielding is relaxing again and I can finally go back to work! As a nurse I've had a real mix of emotions throughout the last year, predominantly spent at home, but the overriding feeling has been guilt. Guilt that my husband has had to work full time then spend hours queuing to buy our family's food each week. Guilty I haven't been able to support colleagues and patients. Guilt that while so many healthcare staff have had to sacrifice so much, I've been safely tucked up at home.

A few months ago my local paper featured me in an article about nurses' pay. If you've seen my social media or read my letters to Boris you'll know it's something I feel very strongly about. I was surprised by how hateful some of the article's comments were towards nurses, stating that we are 'greedy', 'lazy' and that we 'do a pauper's job' so should 'remember our place'. I've since discussed these comments on BBC Essex radio where the DJ was appalled. I've now brushed them off as generalised opinions, made through utter ignorance, by cowardly keyboard warriors who would have no such confidence in reality. But when a comment is a direct personal attack it isn't so easy to forget. A friend of mine who is a successful author said to me recently that she thinks people forget there is an actual human on the other end of their virulent remarks. The article mentioned that the reason I've had to shield is because of a rare lung disease, Chronic Eosinophilic Pneumonia, which is treated with immunosuppressants. It hasn't been a choice of mine to duck out of nursing to have an easy year in the garden. I am at a very real risk of serious complications and I owe it to my family to respond sensibly to Covid. So the comment 'She didn't even work in lockdown' cut deep. It didn't matter to this reader that I've given 24 years of my life so far to nursing, it mattered that I'd had the audacity to fight for my colleagues while I was seemingly swanning around carefree, in her words 'seeking attenshun'.

This made me furious. Firstly, if I'm unable to work, why shouldn't I do what I can to support my colleagues and fight for fair pay and conditions? The original post that caught my local paper's eye was a photo of me taken by my son outside my local MPs office (a photo another hater claimed was fake!). I wanted to raise awareness that, rather than support local healthcare staff, this MP had blocked all contact from nursing groups asking for his help with the *NHS15* campaign. The post garnered so much interest that it had 91,506 positive interactions on Facebook alone. For the support of these people I am so very grateful but the hate from a handful cast a shadow at the time.

Secondly, the reason I was unable to work was actually because of my career. Right at the start of the pandemic when healthcare workers started suffering from Covid themselves a friend of mine said, 'If they're becoming unwell with this, how many healthcare workers have contracted other illnesses in the past?'. His comment hit me like a physical force, because I am one of them. My consultants believe that eight years ago, I was exposed to an unknown substance at work that triggered a response in my body that has lead to lifelong health problems. I won't go into detail about my condition, as I have previously done, but I now have to take long-term steroid medication in both inhaler and tablet form just to function daily. The exhaustion and chest symptoms that overtake me in a flare-up are indescribable and blood tests, X-Rays, bone density scans and CT scans are regular events. However, I've learned to deal with all of this and it really doesn't affect me too badly now I know how to listen to my body. I rarely talk about it in real life as it's just become part of me and that's OK. But when someone accuses me of not pulling my weight during a pandemic, that is not OK.

And there will be plenty of nurses in a similar situation to me. And they are who I am really writing this blog for. Don't feel guilty that you've had to take a year out of your many years of service to stay well enough for more. Don't let other people's opinions weigh you down. Don't feel guilty if having time out has made you realise that nursing isn't for you anymore. The last year has demonstrated only too well how relentlessly tough it is and maybe you've decided you've given all you can. Your colleagues will understand that you've had to make your own health a priority for once. And if you do go back to work, you may just be the person they need to hand the baton to.

County Lines

This was not an easy blog to write but my drive to get this information out there had to supersede any emotions I was feeling. My son has had an inexplicably tough year being the victim of some very dark people. I wasn't sure how he would feel about me writing on this subject so I gave him the blog to read before I posted it anywhere. My heart swelled with pride when he told me to post it because he doesn't want other children experiencing what he has. But my heart also broke for him all over again because I know what he has had to cope with. I can't tell you the strength and resilience this boy has shown. If you don't know about County Lines and you know even just one child, you absolutely must educate yourself. So far this blog has had over 1200 reads.

I want it in this book so that it reaches much further. Nevertheless, if each person who has already read it talks to just one child, then together we have educated an entire senior school population. And that is a great start. If you'd like to help further then please visit any of my social media (details are at the back of the book) and share this blog. It's a pinned post to make it easy to find. I have also included links at the end of this book so that you can read further than just my experience. Getting this subject known and understood is imperative:

County Lines. Maybe you've heard of this, maybe not. But if you are a parent or have children in your life that you care about, it is vital that you learn about it and, most importantly, help to educate these kids by talking about it.

I'd heard of it and thought I had a decent understanding of the subject until recently when my son had, what the police described as, 'a close shave'. I was aware that kids on bikes were targeted for drug running, I was aware that kids who travel in from London by train are a target and I was aware that adults are approaching kids offering to pay for food in return of a favour. These things are happening and if you live pretty much anywhere in England it's most likely happening in your town. But here's what I didn't know and what I feel a responsibility to share. That the people coercing and grooming our kids may well be an adult in a quiet part of the high street, they may well be an adult hanging around the station or chicken shop but what I don't think is publicised widely enough is that they may just as easily be another kid. The same age as yours, in the same class.

The police call this peer grooming and it happens when a 'friend' tries to recruit another child to run packages of drugs or money. These kids are earning around £350-£500 a day so at first it must seem like a great idea. Fast work, fast money. It might not seem that serious at first, but the further up the chain you go, the more deadly it becomes. These gangs think nothing of robbing their own, taking money or drugs from them, so that they become indebted and find it harder and harder to leave this life. These gangs think nothing of using weapons to take down other gangs. These gangs have had kids so trapped that they and their whole family have had to be relocated for safety.

Runners try to convince their peers to work for them. They can be relentless in their efforts to coerce and children who have never been in trouble before may feel increasingly pressured. You might be thinking that your child goes to a good school so you don't need to worry. But the 'good' schools often have more issues around drugs because the kids there are likely to have more money to spend on them. Last year it came to light that my son had become a victim of peer grooming. Thankfully we found out before he got too involved with the boy responsible but even so my son and I received threats, demands for money and I was called in the middle of the night, from a private number, by an anonymous male. I can tell you it's an unnerving experience.

The police and school helped guide us through it and every police officer I spoke to was so supportive and helpful. We were offered an educational visit from two officers so that we and our son could fully understand how County Lines operates and it is terrifying. A teacher accused my son and I of being naïve but after speaking to friends, it turns out that nobody I know had any idea how bad the situation is. Even a friend who was in the Met for 10 years was surprised that it was happening at the school both our sons attend. If, with all of her experience, she was surprised, how are the rest of us supposed to know? I don't disagree that I am naïve about gangland drug wars, as is my son, but isn't that how it should be? Should our kids know about this dark side of life? It breaks my heart to say it but yes. They do need to know because if they don't, they won't see it coming if, and I hope if not when, they are approached to join it.

So please educate yourselves and talk openly to your kids about this. And if you've had a similar experience to mine share it. Maybe your children have been involved on a deeper level but this isn't an issue to be ashamed about. I use the word children because at 14, 15, 16 they really are still children involved in a world far beyond their understanding. And the police know that if they've become involved, they are victims, not criminals. Don't be scared to talk to the police, they understand the system and will work to support your child, not prosecute them. I've included a link which may be the first step to learning more about the business that is County Lines. Please take the time to read about it, maybe speak to your children's school and definitely talk to other parents. We need to protect our children from very real predators.

Mental Un-health

This blog I sat on for a while because I was so worried about upsetting anyone with what I'd written. Mental health is a very sensitive issue so to speak about it regarding children was even more so. I have seen definite changes over the last year in levels of anxiety in adult patients and children alike. What I was witnessing in my role as a school nurse, and especially in my counselling role, caused me to question if we, as a society, are handling such a complex health matter correctly. I have to admit I was scared to read the comments after I posted this but to my great relief I have only had positive feedback from other parents and health professionals who share my concern. See what you think:

Firstly, I feel I need to make some kind of disclaimer to make it clear that what I've written here is in no way intended to offend or upset anyone. I've been sitting on this blog for a couple of months now as the topic is a sensitive one and I've been unsure how well it will be received. It may seem that each paragraph swings between opposing viewpoints and that's because I have no idea what the right outcome should be. I'm not here to give answers as I don't have them but I have had many conversations over the last few months that I feel could raise useful and important discussions. What I have written is based on personal experiences, my own observations and those made by colleagues and other parents.

During my time as a school nurse it has been impossible to ignore how many children seem to be suffering with mental health issues. Stress, anxiety and depression are rife among all year groups and there are days when I wonder if there is a child in existence who is growing up feeling secure in themselves. We all know that the teenage years are difficult. Body changes, body image, independence for the first time, increased school work, exams and, for our current kids, a year of lockdowns doesn't make for an easy ride. But for generations people have been dealing with these changes so why is mental health such a hot topic now? Is it simply because we talk about it more or is it because our children are becoming less and less resilient?

I had a conversation with another school nurse recently about this as we have noticed, particularly in the younger years of senior school, an increased level of mental health needs. I was fascinated by her opinion that resilience is now almost seen as a negative. Her impression is that children are taught to talk about every feeling, thought and emotion but are not encouraged to develop coping strategies to make it through the day. She believes that coping is now seen as a way of merely masking problems. But is it always? I could see her point of view. Absolutely there are children truly suffering and some who have had the most awful childhoods imaginable. However, I believe there are many who are just having what we used to call 'a bad day'. The kind of day that a bubble bath or your favourite chocolate in front of *Friends* used to remedy.

If you've read my blog *County Lines* you'll know that my son has had a terrible few months and we have, of course, encouraged him to talk about everything that has happened. We have also accepted all support on offer from the school and community health team so that he has had every opportunity to process the experience. But we have also discussed his feelings as being a direct response to the threatening behaviour he was a victim of. While of course he will feel low about it, he does not have depression. Over the last month I have seen his mood dramatically improve now that the ordeal is over. He is more applied at school, is spending time creatively and positively and building healthy new friendships. He has learned from the experience and his mistakes and has admitted that talking to me feels like a weight of his chest. So yes, it's obviously great to talk but I feel it's important not to dwell too much but rather look for the positives and see this as a time of progression to help him to move past it. Because although six months of a bad experience seems long at the time, it's a tiny fragment of his whole life.

I've written before about my fondness for the children I care for as a school nurse. I have met some I'd like to do so much more for - those who have a difficult past or present and who haven't had enough care along the way. The effects of this are prevalent in many ways from behaviour, to confidence and school achievements and so much more. But what interests me from my own observations is that the children who have had the worst backgrounds are often the most resilient. These children frequently come to have a chat with me to unload but are usually determined to stay in school. Somehow they have been shaped by what they've been through and are looking towards their future. I am blown away by their attitude and can only admire their perseverance. So why is it then that so many other children attend my medical room every day in an attempt to be sent home?

I frequently see over 60 children a day. That's about 5% of the entire school population on a daily basis and I'd say only a quarter of the children I deal with are genuine. The rest present with all manner of ailments, including anxiety, but don't actually display true symptoms of these. I hear them laughing and chatting to their friends while they're waiting to see me but as soon as they enter my medical room they sink into a suppressed and melancholy state and barely manage to mumble a word to me. They come to see me with the hope that I will send them straight home or, at worst, that I will let them see out their least favourite lesson hiding in the medical room. I've started to wonder – and I know this is controversial - if perhaps we are talking about mental health too much? Could that be possible? These kids are being given very mixed information. Their school sends them the message of resilience and fortitude but they are constantly bombarded by talk of mental health, anxiety, low mood, depression and stress in the media. No wonder they are confused. Their head teacher promotes the idea of committing to schoolwork and building for a future and yet in reality these kids are allowed to sit out of class, listen to music to calm down and I've even heard of a student going to a pet store to have a bit of 'me time' during the school day.

Conversely, the children showing real strength despite the most heart-breaking situations at home sometimes need encouraging to open up. They live in survival mode and their resolve often prevents them from discussing their emotions at all. I've seen two students recently with devastating experiences of varying abuse and have had to encourage them to talk to someone they trust. Sometimes what they're holding inside is too difficult to say out loud and they may not feel ready for a long time. There are days when sowing the seed of the importance of sharing the load is all I can do.

My other question is, does labelling every symptom or emotion actually help a child? I had an interesting discussion with a friend recently whose child has been diagnosed with separation anxiety. After sharing her experience at work, an older colleague suggested that maybe her daughter is just what was once called 'homely'. Kids who just like being at home. After my experience with county lines I'm not sure that being homely is a bad thing at all these days. Does it actually help a child to be labelled as having 'mental health problems'? I was told by a child recently that they have really bad 'maths anxiety'. I instantly reflected on my own time at school when I used to dread my maths lessons and shrink at the back of the class in case I was asked a question. I found maths impossible to grasp and couldn't wait for the lesson to be over. According to this child, I probably had what she called 'maths anxiety' too but because it was never labelled and because lessons were something you went to every day without question I just got on with it.

And that is what we're seeing a real lack of now. Kids who just get on with it. So many colleagues and other parents I talk to are deeply concerned about this and our future as a society. I was talking to another friend of mine whose daughter is having counselling and when I shared this view she said she was so glad I'd said it. In a world where you have to be so cautious expressing opinions I think she'd been worried about feeling this way.

Of course I'm not saying we should go back to the British 'stiff upper lip' way of thinking. Whether you love or hate the Royals, anyone could see that the treatment of William and Harry at their mum's funeral was destined for long lasting repercussions. Repercussions that are evident right now.

Completely suppressing emotions is unhealthy as we all know. I have relatives who have suffered great trauma and loss in their lives and, because of the era this happened in, were not encouraged to talk about it at all from what I gather. My dad lost his dad in a tragic accident when he was just 12 years old and the way it was handled was so different to how it would be today. I'm sure there are millions of adults, particularly men, suffering in silence over events from their past or present. I understand that mental health can be affected by many factors and sometimes there may not even be a clear indicator of why a person is feeling the way they are. Support is essential to help a person understand and deal with their issues but if you've read my blog *Strong* you'll know I believe balance in life is paramount. I'm simply wondering if the subject of mental health has gone too far for our kids? With so many trying to get out of classes claiming their anxiety is the issue are we, by allowing so much time out, actually causing detriment to our children? At the risk of sounding cold, and I should point out here that I treat every single child with care and respect, I do wonder if mental health is becoming an excuse for some children. Definitely not all children but some. On the flip side, I saw a child today who never used to eat at school or do PE because of her anxiety. She told me that she's started to do both of these things. When I asked her what had changed she said "I just told myself to get over it and get on with things'" To be honest this stunned me as it's not an attitude I often see. And I was so happy for her because she exuded a lightness that wasn't there before.

Last month I was speaking to an 87 year old man in my other role as a practice nurse about his health during lockdown. He'd been completely put out by it all as he was forced to stop working for a while. He's since gone back to work and told me he's sick of hearing about mental health in the media. He said "Grow up in the East End during the Blitz and then you'll know about mental health". Obviously this is an extreme viewpoint and I wouldn't wish war as a way of life for any child. But I see his point. His generation wouldn't have seen the school nurse for a paper cut, for bending their finger backwards, for having ink in their hair or for having mud on their trousers. All reasons children have been sent to me. If these kids aren't encouraged to sort this type of problem (and I hesitate to use the word problem here) on their own, how are they ever going face the world of work?

It baffles me when parents repeatedly allow their children to be sent home from school for no real reason. I don't have any power to keep a child in school once the parent has requested this but sometimes I wish I did. I had a mum admit to me just last week that her daughter is a "drama queen" but could I just "pander to her". Again, I had to carry out her wishes but was left wondering what this would achieve. Professionally I feel this makes me look like a total mug and the kids will then expect me to be a complete soft touch at every visit. When a child has overcome a tough day and reached the end of their classes successfully they feel a real sense of achievement. They also usually learn that it really wasn't that bad. If their parents aren't encouraging this kind of staying power then I have no idea how they'll hold a job down in a few years time. Of course every child deserves to be treated with kindness and care and I need to reiterate that I am not intending to make sweeping judgements of all children here. There are those who are in absolute need of appropriate support. But when you're sent over 60 a day to assess, they also need to be seen with discernment to sift out those who are truly suffering and those who are playing the system. As I said at the start, I don't have the answers but I do have increasing concern for our children and their futures.

Yoga

I recently read Claudia Winkleman's book *Quite* where she makes it clear she is not a fan of yoga. She's been known before to describe it as smelling of 'smug and hummus'. While this is amusing, conjuring images of teachers dressed in wheat wafting around an incense filled studio, I actually feel sad that Claudia has never experienced the true benefits of yoga.

If you've read my first book or earlier blogs you'll know that firstly, I suffer with a long-term chest disease, and secondly that I've done yoga for over 20 years now and love it so much I decided to train to teach it in 2018. I've recently read and listened to the experiences of two very successful

YouTube yoga teachers from the channels *Yoga with Bird* and *Sarah Beth Yoga* (both of which I highly recommend if you are looking to practice yoga at home) who have both suffered severe illnesses and for whom yoga has been a vital component of their recovery and management of long-term conditions. It made me consider my own experience and why yoga means so much to me. I rarely get through a day without practising at some point.

It's because it is so healing. Like everybody knows, life can be busy. Work is often hectic, being a working mum is more hectic still and yoga allows time devoted to the present. While yoga does improve strength, flexibility, and overall health, there are times when what you need most is just to be still. It makes you stop while the world continues to whizz by around you. One of the best things about it is being able to develop the ability to relax instantly. It teaches you to go from 60-0 in a matter of moments. When you are living with impaired health you can find yourself pushing on and on to accomplish what's needed for your job, home and family. But there comes a moment when you just have to rest. And restorative yoga is by far the most replenishing way I have found to do this. Of course, this is true for everybody, not just those who have long-term conditions. Another aspect of yoga that I love so much is that it's non-competitive. It's not about keeping up with the teacher or person next to you. And it's not about pushing yourself, it's about listening to your body and meeting its needs on that day regardless of how you've felt practising on other days. It teaches you to be in tune with yourself like no other exercise I have found.

Throughout the pandemic the media has been brimming with advice on mental health, mindfulness, self-care, time out and ways to ease stress and anxiety. I truly believe the best way to accomplish all of this is through yoga. After all, people have been reaping its benefits for centuries. I used yoga breathing techniques to teach children to manage their feelings in lockdown when I was working as a school nurse and counsellor. I noticed a remarkable difference in these kids. And I have had adult students regularly report better sleep, lower stress levels, relief from back and hip pain, improved healing from sports injuries and most importantly in my opinion, a soothed mind.

Yoga makes you notice. It allows you to notice the link between your body and mind and how calming one then calms the other. It allows rest in a culture where doing nothing usually riddles you with guilt.

My cousin lives in Nova Scotia and I remember her saying once that life there seems so much longer than when she lived in the UK. I imagine this is because a slower pace and a more restful, peaceful lifestyle is not frowned upon. Success there isn't measured by how many meetings you can squeeze in between the school run, gym and a quick pit stop to Tesco Express to pick up a fast dinner. Life in Nova Scotia, and other places I have been to, is absorbed and noticed. It's not something that passes by in a hurry because of a need to cram a day full of activities which, when we look back, won't actually matter. I have a great aunt in Australia who has said she sometimes spends a whole day reading a good book. What a wonderful way to spend precious time.

If you feel you need to soothe your mind and body from the pressures of a chaotic society and haven't already, try yoga. You may need to try a few different classes and teachers to find what suits you best (something I suspect Claudia didn't do!) and if you want to try a live class at home with nobody watching just drop me a message ☺

Informed

This I wrote after being extremely alarmed at the amount of nonsensical propaganda I was seeing on all forms of social media, written by completely unqualified members of the public trying to persuade others to discard their masks and run like lightning from vaccines. I fully respect the decision to choose whether you want to be vaccinated or not. But if you are so furiously promoting the avoidance of the vaccine, surely you are no different to those who are suggesting the vaccine as a good and sensible option? And I must say, the experts promoting the vaccine are most certainly doing so in a more professional manner than the angry posts I have seen.

*

The Covid vaccine and masks. Subjects I am spoken to about on a daily basis at work and out of it. I have even been tagged on Instagram in debates about whether it should be mandatory for healthcare workers to be vaccinated or not. My opinion is that the vaccine should be a personal choice and I don't think any government should have the power to impose medication of any sort on a person. My opinion on masks is that unless you have a truly valid medical reason for not wearing one, what possible harm can it do to put one on when required? The point of them is to stop the spread from you, not to you, and I think wearing one shows that you respect those around you. Choosing not to simply because you don't like it isn't an excuse. What is important when deciding whether to have the vaccine or not, regardless of your profession, is that your sources of information are trustworthy and reliable. I'm sure anti-vaxxers will step in here and tell me that the government are not providing this kind of information. And I will have to leave you to decide whether you believe that or not but I would say medical research is the best place to educate yourself to enable you to make an informed choice.

I fully respect the decision not to have the vaccine as long as it's an informed one. I didn't immediately leap to the decision to have it myself since it's such a new vaccine. It wasn't until I had completed the training to administer it and come to understand the science behind it that I felt comfortable enough to have it. I also appreciate that deciding to have it yourself is one thing but that making the choice to give it to your children is another entirely. I spoke to my children who are 15 and 12 and allowed them to be part of the decision too. They have both opted to go for it but I appreciate it's a tough one.

You've probably seen recently that celebrities are joining in the debate. Jennifer Aniston has actually cut off her friends who won't have the vaccine or reveal if they've been vaccinated or not. Her argument is that she wants to know if she comes into contact with someone who may have the virus so that she can avoid passing it on to others more vulnerable. She said "It's tricky because everyone is entitled to their own opinion - but a lot of opinions don't feel based on anything except fear or propaganda."

And this is what horrifies me - the amount of status updates, memes and arguments on Facebook and other social media platforms apparently proving that the vaccine is harmful or ineffective or a conspiracy. And by the way, if you're writing a meme hoping to convince people of anything, please check your spelling! The amount I've seen written incoherently is hilarious.

Nicki Minaj recently claimed that the vaccine can make men impotent. This even caused England's chief medical officer Chris Whitty to step in and speak about her claim. He said that Nicki "should be ashamed" after she tweeted an unfounded story about a man who'd been given the vaccine and then apparently became impotent. During a news conference at Downing Street he said "There are a number of myths that fly around, some of which are just clearly ridiculous and some of which are clearly designed just to scare. That happens to be one of them." He also said that there are "people that go around trying to discourage other people from taking a vaccine which could be life-saving or prevent them from having life-changing injuries to themselves".

I'm not saying you must or mustn't get the vaccine, the choice is yours. But please make sure your sources are accurate and reliable, not from some anti-vaxxer hothead with no real medical knowledge splashing their unsubstantiated opinions all over social media.

I'll leave you with my favourite tweet on the subject of masks which I feel demonstrates my point perfectly:

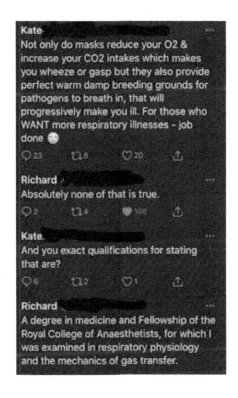

Kate
Not only do masks reduce your O2 & increase your CO2 intakes which makes you wheeze or gasp but they also provide perfect warm damp breeding grounds for pathogens to breath in, that will progressively make you ill. For those who WANT more respiratory illnesses - job done 😴

💬 23   🔁 8   ♡ 20   ⬆️

Richard
Absolutely none of that is true.

💬 2   🔁 4   ♥ 106   ⬆️

Kate
And you exact qualifications for stating that are?

💬 6   🔁 2   ♡ 1   ⬆️

Richard
A degree in medicine and Fellowship of the Royal College of Anaesthetists, for which I was examined in respiratory physiology and the mechanics of gas transfer.

Genuine

I wrote this blog after reflecting on recent events where I live and after considering how people live on after death:

My hometown has been a place of tragedy over the last few months. Several people have lost their lives through acts of violence, the most well-known being the unfathomable and futile stabbing of Sir David Amess. Add to these events loss in my personal life and the subject of death has been impossible to avoid.

It is only natural for such harrowing experiences to highlight the fragility of life – a subject that also cannot be avoided when living with a chronic disease – but rather than be depressed by the fallible nature of what it is to be human, I have felt an overwhelming need to make sure my life has a lasting effect when I'm gone.

I was listening to one of my favourite artists Tori Amos at the weekend and one of her newest songs references her mother's death. She sings of the way her mother is described by others in what is a truly beautiful and moving song. And it made me hope that when I am no longer here, there will be people who talk fondly about me to my children. I want them and those closest to me to have minds bursting with colourful memories of me. I've always tried my best, as most mothers do, to ensure my children have an abundance of happy times throughout childhood. Times they can still laugh about when they are much older. And if they're laughing about me, then so be it. I've also tried to teach them to be genuine – to be who you really are, with whoever you're with. This is something they have both said they've noticed about me recently so I'm pleased this message is making its way through.

My dad was fairly recently told stories about his dad that he had never heard before. Some of them he wouldn't have known at the time as he was only 12 when his dad died so never knew him through an adult's eyes. From what I have seen, read and been told, my grandad was a very unusual character, regularly making the news for his designs and contributions to the world of homebuilt aircraft. He didn't let anyone trample on his dreams and certainly let his genuine personality shine through, as unconventional as it was. So much so that even though my grannie, his wife, was only 45 when he died, she never married again. I once asked why and she simply replied that she would have never found another man to match him. He gave her a life filled with fun, flights in Tiger Moths and an aeroplane fuselage in their first-floor lounge while he built his first plane! She was exceptionally tolerant of his mad professor ways. It has often been said that he left a remarkable legacy through his work in aviation.

More wonderful still is that, even decades after his death, his family and friends are still talking about him and laughing about their times together. Surely that, although cut tragically short, was a life well lived. And surely that is a true legacy.

Respect

As with the blog *Mental Un-health,* I've
been cautious to publish this one. I
wrote it on a day when, quite clearly,
I'd had enough. I was tired of the
treatment I was receiving from certain
doctors at work – not all doctors I
must add – and some patients. I've
read it and re-read it and have decided
that sometimes you have to let your
honest feelings out and these are
mine. This isn't me whining after a
bad day but explaining the reasons I
often feel so dissatisfied in a difficult
and responsible job. Again I feel I
need to make a disclaimer that I
absolutely do not have anything
against teachers or carers. They are
both vital careers which I respect, it's
just that they and we as nurses are
often compared in the media since we
are all in the public sector. I am

merely using my experience of working in a school and healthcare to make some comparisons myself:

For quite a while now I've found it hard to settle in a job for longer than a couple of years. This didn't used to be the case, I worked at one surgery for 16 years so I know it's not because I don't have staying power. It's taken me a long time to work out what it is I am searching for in a job and then a few incidents last week caused me to realise. It's the simple act of respect. Not because I want to be seen as better than anyone else, but because I just want to be recognised as the professional that I am and treated equally to other colleagues. I believe this lack of respect, particularly through a pandemic, is partly why we have seen such a rise in the number of nurses fighting for fairer pay and conditions. We are just too tired to carry on as we are.

I can't explain why but nurses so often seem to be the bottom of the pile. Patients frequently treat us like their personal servants while doctors are seen as some sort of god.

I left my job as a school nurse in the summer because, despite repeated requests for change, I was seeing scores of children who had been sent by the teachers simply because they wanted them out of the class. Many of them were not ill and I am convinced that, after speaking to friends who are teachers, sending them to the school nurse was the easy option if they were disrupting the class. I must point out that not all teachers did this, some only sent children to me who were obviously genuinely unwell and would, when possible, escort them down themselves. And my manager was the most supportive, approachable and understanding I have ever had, she just couldn't possibly control how other staff viewed me. However, there was still a huge proportion of children who were clogging up the medical room for no reason, limiting and delaying the time I could spend with those who truly needed me. This made me feel that I was being treated as a lesser member of staff by some teachers. Again, I must reiterate not all. In addition to this, I was paid as support staff when I am just as qualified as the teachers and have many more years' experience than some. This meant that despite working the same hours and seeing around 60 children a day, I was paid around £10k pro rata less than my colleagues. Even when I was working almost full time at the school, I had to work extra clinics in general practice to top up my salary. In the end this caused my chest condition to flare up and I had to leave this job because I needed to put my health first and simply couldn't afford to stay. I do not blame my management for my pay scale but the wider education system. For some reason whoever is at the top thought it was ok to seek a qualified nurse for a role but pay them less than deserved.

I have since returned to practice nursing but am still finding a distinct lack of respect in the way I am treated by some. I arrived to work last week to find that a GP had been using my room to see patients. Obviously I have no problem with this ordinarily as many doctors I have worked with have treated me with respect and in some cases, have really had my back.

But what I found on my desk was a used tongue depressor, used ear covers for an otoscope and used wrappers from single use equipment. Today I came into work to find similar except the doctor's discarded breakfast was added to the mix. Why is this acceptable? I sanitise my desk at the start and end of every surgery and do not expect to be treated as a little woman who will come in and clean up after the doctor. The nurse is so often treated as a less deserving member of staff and I simply cannot understand the root of this.

And while many patients are nothing but lovely, there remain some who seem to see nurses as a lower form of species. Two weeks ago a patient was waiting for her appointment and was told by the receptionist that she needed to wear a mask in a healthcare setting. The patient replied that she would wear one when she saw the doctor. The receptionist advised her that she would also need to wear one to see me to which she disdainfully replied 'Even for the nurse?'. How can this be ok? Why do I not deserve to be treated as a fellow human being? I have previously written and spoken on the radio about being told by a cowardly keyboard warrior that if I choose a 'pauper's job' I should 'remember my place'. What place is that exactly?

I recall once being at a wedding surrounded by doctors feeling like Bridget Jones in the scene where she's at a party surrounded by lawyers. The woman next to me was explaining to her friend that she and her family were horrified that her sister was choosing to train as 'just' a nurse over a career in medicine. After a while she turned to me and asked what it was I do. I nonchalantly replied that I am 'just a nurse'.

And this lack of respect goes much further than pay alone. I've had to consistently work in conditions with no breaks, faulty or no equipment - and I am talking real basics here such as bedroll, heating and a working printer. I have campaigned for better pay and conditions over the last year and have been spoken to by teachers who have told me that they haven't had a pay rise for quite some time either. The difference is that teachers are already paid quite a lot more than nurses with notoriously better working hours and holiday. Nurses' starting salary is around £5-6k less than a teacher's starting salary. And by the way, I am not intending to bash teachers here. I have seen first-hand what a relentless and difficult job it is and teachers deserve every penny. My argument is simply that so do we.

The other argument that has come up time and time again during the *NHS15* campaign is that carers deserve to be paid similarly to nurses. I started my career working in care and I know what an exhausting and thankless job it is. I absolutely agree that carers should be paid far more than the minimum wage. However, the point that is always missed here is that nurses are professionals. We have to have degrees and the level of responsibility is far higher than that of a carer. So I disagree that we should be paid on a similar level. Yes carers should definitely be paid more but if they are paid the same as nurses, there is no recognition of, or incentive to undergo the gruelling training nurses have to complete in order to earn their registration.

I have now been offered a new job in a completely different healthcare setting which I am truly excited about. However I am trying not to get too carried away as I have been in this place of optimism many times before and have repeatedly been let down. The new year will mark 20 years since I qualified and I have made the decision that this is a last ditch attempt at finding a job in nursing that doesn't make me feel a lesser citizen. If this doesn't work out I'll be looking for a complete career change. But I would love to find the working conditions I've been looking for and sincerely hope I never have to write the book 'Blue Girl: Nursing No More'.

Media

Speaking at *NHS15* rally in September 2020.

Blue Girl Nurse
21 Oct 2020 · 🌐

···

To the five haters I had on my last post I say this. You may not think you know anyone who has used food banks but consider that those who've had to, probably wouldn't tell you. That moment in their lives wouldn't have been a proud one but one when they realised they needed help. We will all need help of some kind in our lives and there is no shame in accepting it in desperate times.

From my work as a nurse in the community, surgeries and a school I know that hard times have fallen on people unexpectedly and more people than you think have had to rely on the kindness of others, thankfully often just for a short time.

These people are not greedy, as one person suggested nurses are, or lazy. They are real people often with children who are doing their best.

I'm sure I'll get more judgemental and spiteful comments on here but I'm very happy to see that those people are a tiny minority. If Covid has taught me anything it's that we need to uphold each other more than ever.

And to the 91506 people who have seen, liked, shared or commented positively on my post, I truly thank you for supporting our fight.

Facebook post in response to hateful comments.

Blue Girl Nurse

4 Jan · 🌐

· · ·

Thinking of teachers today. What a job to go back to after the government's string of disorganised and chaotic decisions. Thank you for everything you do ⭐

Post showing I have nothing against teachers!

Bluegirlnurse
@bluegirlnurse

Replying to @ZacEfron and @ZekeFinnMusic

The people of Rainham will be delighted by this tweet. I loved that you just showed up to help with a litter pick. Imagine being those teenage girls who'd volunteered, must've made their year! To be fair it would make my year and I'm 39! Really great show, very well done.

10:38 · 05 Aug 20 · Twitter for Android

My tweet on *Down to Earth*

Zac Efron liked your reply

The people of Rainham will be delighted by this tweet. I loved that you just showed up to help with a litter pick. Imagine being those teenage girls who'...

And the like that made my day!

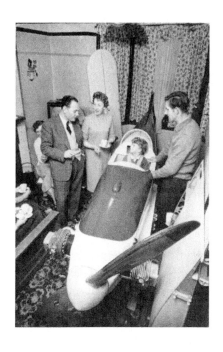

Photo showing my grandad John Taylor *right* and my dad Terry sitting in the fuselage of the Taylor Monoplane in their lounge which I referred to in *Genuine*.

Photo from the news at the time showing part of the Taylor Monoplane being taken out of the first floor lounge window!

A family legacy I am immensely proud of. If you're interested in this remarkable story visit www.taylortitch.co.uk or watch the story here;

https://www.youtube.com/watch?v=8jpqw0IWRww

Links Regarding County Lines

https://www.seethesigns.org.uk/

https://www.childrenssociety.org.uk/what-we-do/our-work/child-criminal-exploitation-and-county-lines/what-is-county-lines?gclid=EAIaIQobChMI96-C64CO9AIVUevtCh2YWgvjEAAYASAAEgI06PD_BwE

https://www.railwaychildren.org.uk/get-involved/campaigns/its-not-always-easy-to-see-when-children-are-in-danger/?gclid=EAIaIQobChMI96-C64CO9AIVUevtCh2YWgvjEAAYAiAAEgJIPPD_BwE

Acknowledgements

Thanks of course, to my family and friends for all their support since *Blue Girl: Nursing Beyond the Ward*. And for endlessly listening to me talk about that book, its progress and this new one!

Thanks to my blog readers for their continued support and comments.

Special thanks to my author friend Lizzie Page who has been so encouraging and kind as I have embarked on this writing journey. Please check out her books, they are completely fabulous and will have you hooked.

And huge thanks to my readers who have bought, downloaded and reviewed *Blue Girl: Nursing Beyond the Ward*. Although very different, I hope you enjoy *Blue Girl: Nursing From Home*. Thank you for making contact with me and giving such lovely feedback. Despite huge imposter syndrome, I continue to be blown away by your kindness and support.

x

If you would like to follow me, you can find me @bluegirlnurse on Instagram and Twitter and my Facebook page Blue Girl Nurse.

Any reviews, of either book, will be greatly appreciated.

Printed in Great Britain
by Amazon

23359589R00067